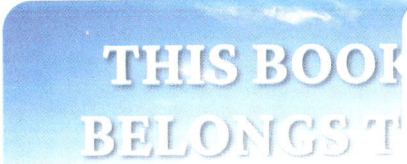

Cynthia Wicht

Gathering the Quiet

Gathering the Quiet

Thos. R. Hines

Copyright © 2023 by Thos. R. Hines

All rights reserved.

This book or any portion thereof may not be reproduced or used in any manner whatsoever without the express written permission of the author except for the use of brief quotations in a book review.

Contact the author at:
fridayletters48@gmail.com

Printed in the United States of America

First Printing, 2023

ISBN 9798388473950

Cover design by Kerry Hines LaCross

Interior design by Debora McNeer

Author photo by Jennifer Ragone Hines
Permission granted for use of logo by Kubota USA

In memory of
David W. Hatch
And
Edward J. Farrell

Table of Contents

PART ONE
Friday Letters to God

I 1
Winter Expectation
Expectations 3
Reel 4
Name..................................5
Half-a-moon 6
Bystander 7
Commandment..................8
Acorn..................................9
Stopper............................10
Squeaky............................11
Body..................................12
Earth 13
Pinned 14
Monday 15
Truer 16
As If 17
Wisp 18

II 19
Spring Awareness
Spile 21
Shepherd..........................22
Melt..................................23
Ant 24
Bug....................................25

Pace..................................26
Blessed 27
Sleeve 28
Seeds................................29
Spring 30
Hold On 31
Grow 32
Tree 33
Nudge 34

III 35
Building House with Grandson
House 37
Nod 38
Foundation 39
Ode to a Circular Saw 40
Slab 41
Feast 42
Build................................43
Stops By 44

IV..................................45
Bride and Dog
Smile of God 47
Shoes and Dogs...............48
Issues 49
Glimpse 50
Rest 51
Joyfully 52

V..53
Along the Way
Bridge..........................55
Minus 2 56
BookClub......................57
Sprinter 58
Woodchuck....................59

VI...61
Glimpses of God
Mereness 63
Knock 64
Sit................................65
Sticks...........................66
Lower Case...................67
Sometimes....................68
Chapel..........................69
Towardness 70
Ineffability....................71
Happiness.....................72
Thin..............................73
Theologizing 74
Shards 75

VII 77
Wisdom, Presence, Gratitude
Imprinted 79
Wiggling.......................80
Washed........................81
Constantly 82

Minus 3 83
Day Begins 84
Brother Ass...................85
Formless 86
Shimmering..................87
Happiness (part 2) 88
Four Fragments 89
Letters To God 90

PART TWO
Friday Rx

I..95
Longing
Sadness 97
Relief...........................98
Battery 99
Lunch 100
Lawn 101
Pouch 102
Driveway.....................103
Temple 104
Ponder........................105
Out.............................106
Whisper......................107
Grace..........................108
Morning Damp.............109
Wind 110
Flow 111

II 113
Along the Way
Gift 115
Her Face 116
Box Store Girl................117
Old Fellows 118
Jelly..................................119
Drummer........................120
Raggedy 121
St. Pat's Day
   in North Carolina 122
Holyday..........................123
Firewood 124
Up North 125
Green Apples.................126
Egg 127
Barefoot Waterski..........128
Away 129
Grandchildren 130
Juxtaposition..................131
Fall 132
Oak 133
Timothy (2016)..............134
The Day..........................136
Wonderful 137
Acorns 138
Career 139
Hummingbird................140
Grandma Gail................141
Side Altar 142
Christmas 1952 143

Subscribe........................144
Kiss..................................145
Rubbing..........................146
Stone Wall......................147
Bacon 148
Growing Pains 149
Apologies to William 150
Summer 1959.................151
Weld................................152
Memorial........................153
Columbine.....................154
Carrot..............................155
Back Home 156
Going Back 157
High School Wrestling...158
Brownies 160
Parts 161
Travel 162
Buddy..............................163
Voice................................163
New Glasses 166
Someone's Daughter......167

III 169
Calling Out God
Out of Order..................171
Prayer..............................172
Embrace Goodness 173
Forgiveness.....................174
Holy Visit........................175
Lifted...............................176

Early Morning Grouch ...177
Help ...178
Sleepless on the
   Western Slopes ...179
Yard ...180
Woodchuck ...181
Megan and Jake ...182
Omega, N.Y. ...183
Heroic Myth ...184
Paint ...185
When We Were Younger ...186
Quandary ...187
Tipping ...188
Jump ...189
Some ...190
Better ...191
Stick ...192
When ...193
Body ...194
Altar ...195
The Trek ...196
Why ...197
Lauds and Vespers ...198
Tossed ...199

IV ...201
Wife
Teacup ...203
Orphans by the Sink ...204
Slip Off ...205
Together ...206
Be ...207
Autumn Morning ...208
Wednesday ...209
Famousness ...210
Anniversary 45 ...211
Nesting ...212
Communication ...213

V ...215
On Writing
Poems ...217
Bread ...218
Spilled Soup ...219
Words and Meaning ...220
Of One ...221
Veil ...222
January ...223
15 February ...224
Morning Quiet ...225
Veni Creator ...226
Awareness ...227

VI ...229
Awareness
Desiderata ...231
Lost ...232
Loss ...233
Beams ...234
Towardness ...235
Granddaughter on
   Her Second Birthday ...236

Clippings	237	Traps	250
Cables	238	Inertia	251
Trees	239	Letting Go	252
Attend	240	Current	253
Compost	241	Illusion	254
Moment	242	Form and Formless	255
Table	243	Before (Exodus and Jeremiah)	256
Some	244		
Toll	245	Staying	257
Fortune	246	Grace	258
Before	247	Positing Faith	259
Falls Away	248	Grandson on Lap	260
Clinkers	249	Each	261

Gathering the Quiet

I was born on Halloween 1948 in Ann Arbor, Michigan. In grade school I went to catechism in Quonset huts at St. Alexis in Willow Run, not far from the WWII Bomber Plant. The Sisters knew everything about God. One summer I had to memorize a mimeographed truth each day before I could go out and play baseball.

Later, with degrees in philosophy and theology, I earned my living in the construction industry.

In 2015, I wrote a note to several friends and sent it out on a Friday morning. One of them, Martha, wrote back saying it was a good Friday Rx for her. The readership grew and the practice continued on Fridays for the next three years.

In 2020, still not comfortable with the management of creation (so much 'noise') and still not satisfactorily 'knowing', I began writing and sending Friday Letters To God, predawn ponderings, calling, wondering, cajoling, trying to say what is unsayable. The response has been favorable.

Let's start with Friday Letters To God, gathering the Quiet.

Thos. R. Hines
Autumn 2022
Irish Hills, Michigan

*"People don't come to church
for preachments, of course,
but to daydream about God."*
– Kurt Vonnegut

PART ONE
FRIDAY LETTERS TO GOD

I
WINTER EXPECTATION

Expectations

My brother writes
'You expect a lot from God'

I don't know what to expect
I don't know whether to pray for rain
or get off my ass and invent irrigation
Or just let it be

What if I run away and hide
ignoring sadness and turmoil
What if I cry out 'Lord Lord'

What if a happy dog licks my face
and I not take self so seriously
this cold winter morning

Reel

Dear God

What shall You do of me

still soft clay after many years

a Spirit dangling as if by cable

like a marionette, clop clop

on wooden floor

acting the fool

a well-intentioned hobo carrying

too large a backpack

Reel me in

Name

Dear God

Will you warm me in sun

Will you lend certitude

Another day, another cup

Another beggar at the off-ramp

Teach me to navigate the

prickery path

What is your name

Is it 'Yes'

Half-a-moon

Dear God

Is it okay to give you a call

this pre-dawn with

half-a-moon clear in the sky

Could you send sun to melt winter

and warm each bluebird egg

Melt me gently

to fertile soil

Bystander

Dear God

I, your guilty bystander, clueless,

entranced

Shall life be a moment of beauty

Or a stew of coming-to-be

Commandment

Dear God

Pre-dawn

Will light light the way soon enough

Will coffee make for optimism

What can be said that is true

Can word and symbol be trusted

Lend comfort to the afflicted

Walk humbly with God

Acorn

Dear God

Like a lost shoe

Where are you

Shall I ring bells and light candles

Sit in supplication

walk the dog

clean the bathroom

Maybe I should shrink into the

space of an acorn

into the place-less Heart of God

Stopper

Dear God

I rarely talk about you

(as if I knew what to say)

You're kind of a conversation stopper

who's leaked in since childhood

rattling around

finding place

You don't text

People dress You in silly clothes

I sit in quiet

Waiting, trying to be open

Squeaky

Dear God

Come into the moment

Cool overheated self

Wash away sweaty opinion and judgment

Spread Knowing as if from an oil can to our

squeaky hearts

as we wake from the sleep

of unknowing

Body

Dear God
This body
A wonderment
A mystery

Hover near
flow the juices
lend Joy and Gratitude
Bless our unknowing

Earth

Dear God
Go ahead, heal the earth
All this reckless consumption

I recall Mother Teresa in an interview
in Detroit in 1978
was asked what *should we do*
She replied that, first, we should pray that
Earth be not worse from our being here

Pinned

Dear God

Your realm so large

So many zip codes to manage

How will you find me

and keep me pinned to your jacket

like a flower at the eighth-grade dance

Monday

Dear God

Monday morning

I don't feel like talking

You okay with that?

You, standing by your holy ironing board

in an old bathrobe, cigarette dangling from lips

(Paint that on the chapel ceiling)

(I thought you were going to quit)

Okay, let's have coffee

But don't talk

just for a while

Truer

Dear God

On a winter morn

this pesky noisy self

like an unruly scratching puppy

Cute, but …

Empty me of me

Lend Truer Vessel

As If

Dear God
Amidst kaleidoscope of rattle
Come
Clear my sight

Guide these well-aged arms
(Only an eye's blink from
childhood sandbox)
Still digging, tossing sand, working
as if an ant or bee
As if

Wisp

Dear God

Let me hide in the folds of your skirt

Unable to invent satisfactory self

puzzle pieces imprecise

chain not fitting on sprocket

This 'me' invention, so fragile

Potter's clay wobbling on Your wheel

A touch please, a wee wisp

II
SPRING AWARENESS

Spile

Dear God

Your moon is a third now

Visible between slim branches

light at dawn

All that phloem and xylem

we learned about in tenth grade

How much shall I invent

and how much comes

from Truer Source

May we tap it like the maple tree

Wisdom drip-dripping from the spile

and then cook it down

renaming it 'Grace'

Shepherd

Dear God

Teach this marionette to dance

this wooden boy to be true

this restless child the way home

to the palm of your hand

into your vest pocket

onto the tip of your tongue

Language and symbol

to say what is not sayable

Each calls to God

in word and gesture unique

according to longings of heart

Send the slightest shepherd

a flower, a bee, a word

to lead us home

Melt

Dear God how is it
we assign you human features: arms, legs
rules, tyrannical behavior

Perhaps you are
'beyond' human assignment
Yet 'knowable'
like the sun at dawn-
far enough not to melt us
close enough to melt us

Ant

Dear God
A good day to walk Earth
treading gently
aware of bounty
not consuming
not disrupting

When we are little boys
a constant occupation
is to scuff ant hills, to mess
neatly formed sand mounds
Or better yet, to pee on them
There, a nice lake for you Mr. Ant

Now, an old guy
I refrain
from disrupting tiny nations

Bug

Dear God

What *are* we this morning

this you/me

Are we hotdog/mustard

distinct but co-mingling

Invisible surface tension

me a bug on your pond?

Pace

Tread gently in your wanderings

God sits in a tiny cart along the way

Turtle, up from wetlands

tows God-cart in warming sun

at a pace known only to Turtle and God

Blessed

Dear God

Blessed be the frozen dawn

Blessed awakening

Blessed the deer low in wetlands

Blessed be busy hands and sunlight

Surely our hearts will thaw

Surely we will rise and mix batter

This is the day the Lord has made

Let us rejoice and be glad

Sleeve

Dear God

May we be true with resources

Not greedy or wasteful

Let us not foul the air

Let us be healers

May we tread lightly

May You wear us on your sleeve

Seeds

Saturday dawn
Four deer slow-walk in lowlands
mere shadows blending in
mounds of sedge grass
past mid-February
Winter's back broken
Soon maple sap will flow

Dear God
May I write you a card
As you have written me
Word and sound
color and shape
touch and scent
seeds of spring

Spring

Dear God

Baby leaves of the big elm

chilly at first sun

The oak holding back

Sweet cherry readying to burst white flower

honeybee's delight

On the ground brave hepatica

like shy seventh graders up to dance

Violets quick to follow

Spring peepers

Turtles in the driveway

We enter Garden

where we cannot but uncinch

our hungry hungry Heart

Hold On

Dear God
On a snowy April day
Flowers wearing wintry shawls
Young leaves in chilly white teepees

Hold on
just a few hours
Let the sun butter your toast

Grow

Dear God

Shall we contemplate creation

Or play with goofy dog

Yes

Canopy outside forming, greening

readying to protect southern exposure

in heat of summer

Sometimes we walk in clover and orange flowers

Sometimes in mud

Be wakened

"Plants want to grow" (Edwin King)

Tree

Tree as art and beauty

Takes sun and makes shade

Takes waste and makes mass

Bares wings to God, smiles upon the sky

Anchors to earth, sipping and sharing with a thousand tiny tongues

The home and future home of countless species

Each in turn, for a while

Nudge

Even if we are bathed in Light
Even if Bliss attaches for days
like a chigger bite,
still we walk dusty gravel,
deerflies relentless
Complete, yet somehow incomplete
Content but longing

Wild raspberries not so strong this year
But *here* at the edge of wetlands
an unexpected bush lush of blackberries
Tactile awareness like a pricking branch
The God of Humor nudges
again and again

III
BUILDING HOUSE WITH GRANDSON

(Note: I'm building a house for son out front on an acre by the road. I suspect it will come up in these Friday letters.)

House

Dear God

Building a house

Rearranging dirt, what did you hide down there

undisturbed these eons

for me to hit with steel shovel

Sand and gravel from glacier

Am I building a house

or trying to be found

To Know and to be Known, to

lose separation

Nod

Dear God

Builder of houses

Can an old guy do it once more

Body and confidence shaky

Shoulders throb after one day

Actually, feels kinda good …

Kiss-my-ass you aches and pains

God-in-a-nail-pouch

Let this house be *art*

Lend the slightest gesture

a nod in this direction

Strap it on

Foundation

Dear God

Sunny day

Frost-laws off

Giant concrete truck belching like a greedy dinosaur

Trench walls holding

to welcome tons

of slush soon solid

to carry the load

May the yoke be easy, the burden light

Ode to a Circular Saw

I've a house to build

Shall I order a new Skil Worm Drive,

Mine wore out after thirty years

She looks to most

large and cumbersome

an oversized locomotive, blade on the left

To those of us grown up with her,

she is machinery art

on the job of any knowing carpenter

or tool snob.   Yeah!

Slab

Dear God

Pouring floor slab in a couple hours

Grandson sleeping in loft

Dog stirring, coffee dripping

A good crew coming

Unforgiving concrete

always a risk it will misbehave

like a two-year-old at the grocery store

May old guy boots lift spritely

in heavy cement

like springtime fawns

one more time

(next day)

(five old men and a thirteen year old, floor near perfect!)

Feast

Dear God

On Saturday morn

Successful work yesterday, body ache

Good ache

Grandson sleeps in loft

Dog rests at foot

Bride sips coffee at southern window

It needn't get better

Resting in the quiet Heart of God

Enough is a Feast

Build

If I forget Thee Lord let my tongue cleave to my palate
Work looms, a house to build
Wood finding place as walls and roof
stoutly connect to concrete base
Fenestration offering light and passage
Three-dimensional order from flat surface
separation of inside from outside
House takes shape, possibility of *home*

Stops By

The Oriole stops by for grape jelly
squawking loudly at the empty vessel
I up and spoon her a healthy dollop
Her song sweeter as
dog sidles up for morning love

Brother stops by from North Carolina
to help
We'll sheath the roof
20-ounce hammers and a worm drive saw
It will take a few sheets to regain
the rhythm we had fifty years ago
before OSB and nail guns

IV
BRIDE AND DOG

Smile of God

Dear God

On a Sunday dawn

Dog and bride asleep

She must have stayed up late

A pecan pie sits at stove top

mysterious art

And jars of maple syrup

lined in rows, sealed for storage

Each drop, drop, drop

gathered at tree

harvest of Gift

affirmation

merged with toil

and cooking-down

The crooked smile of God

Shoes and Dogs

Dear God

What is the greatest commandment

while drinking coffee

awaiting the dog and

bride to rise

Are we different after fifty years

Gone through a bunch of shoes and dogs

some houses

Still adjusting and cooking down

Trying to diminish pesky ego

The greatest commandment?

Try to be good

don't be a jerk

be generous

open heart vault

embrace all as One

Issues

Dear God

All these issues

Do I have enough cream for coffee

Does the dog stink

Should she be on the couch

Will the oak buds survive

Will the bee find pollen

Will you come around if I don't assign you a face

a name, a purpose

Are you

the place between artist's brush and paint

the quiet between raindrops

How can I *not be* of You

Glimpse

Dear God

Years ago my bride insisted I put a window

high on the south wall

Grumbling, I did so

How did she know You would put your large moon

there, above, to greet me early morning?

A window peeking into Heart, a glimpse of Light

as You whisper, *'Before you were in your mother's womb, I know you'*

Rest

Dear God

Mind spooling

Scrolling countless concerns

All this noise

Day of rest

A not unreasonable tradition

The dog, meditation walk, unhurried

Reach out

Allow kindness to fill the vessel

Joyfully

Dear God

Are you the Joy of wife and dog

chatting about breakfast,

abundantly accepting and endlessly forgiving

Are You like that

Accepting, forgiving

May wind be gentle

the sunrise warm

May Your smile find us

May kindness fill our hearts and heal wounds

May we dance Joyfully with wife and dog of morning

V
ALONG THE WAY

Bridge

Dear God

If I couldn't sleep

I'd get in the truck at 4:30 a.m.

and drive to the all-night restaurant

I'd write a letter to my mom in Florida

on a paper placemat

I'd send cash for her bridge tournament

She hasn't had mail in twenty years

The grimy eatery gone

Who will take my call in the uncertain hours

Minus 2

Dear God

Minus 2 at 7:00 a.m.

Do I need commas?

Do I need boots and gloves, an igloo

Do I need a project or better knees

What signals 'enough'

Shall I change jobs

Shall I sit at sidewalk in Paris, penniless

and drink bitter coffee and smoke bitter cigarettes,

borrow paint or clay from hungover friends

Chilly thoughts
    Signed, Crusty Old Guy

BookClub

Dear God

A weekend North

with BookClub, our thirty-fifth year

Six of us now

A lot of books and babies

Some heartache and loss

Still good energy and voice

generous sharing

amidst wine and beer-soaked interruptions

kindness and acceptance

unless you choose a stinker or

didn't read the book

At table, a wisp of prayer, a grand meal

We start earlier and end

when signaled by a member napping

on the floor

BookClub

Sprinter

It is not important that your granddaughter
win the race

What is important is that you wait in the windy
bleachers

while she huddles with her seventh-grade
teammates

She sees you, that smile, she waves

She runs

Her time in the 100-meter sprint

clearly under a minute

Woodchuck

I've been peeing each day into the woodchuck hole

under the ramp of the garden shed

Not a neighborly gesture

though less aggressive than trapping or shooting

We're not yet to where

the wolf shall dwell with the lamb

It's asparagus season, maybe the woodchuck
will move out

VI
GLIMPSES OF GOD

Mereness

Dear God

I've a life-long suspicion that You *Are*

that there is something *right* about You

that You self-reveal on your own schedule

and cherish the mereness of humanity

Knock

Dear God, why are some
pretty in middle-school, while others
amble around the edge of pain
in shoes from the cheap store
How come some feel good and some
are crushed
Do we make this up

Maybe we *choose* to participate
only to find the prize soft
'That's it?'

Later we return to the
basement-door-of-god
We knock
God whispers
Come in, Come in

Sit

Dear God, dare I seek you

Sun breaking

warming Sunday morn

Wanting to sit on the porch with you

What is Your desire

Only my heart?

All You want is to sit with me?

Wow! Sure

Sticks

Dear God

How is it that each morning

all existence is shaken

like a box of pick-up sticks

then re-strewn

in disorder

How about it, this messy pile

Can't You just take it away

When one tired mom or grandma

cares for a child

it profoundly reshapes All Creation

Lower Case

I don't mean to be disrespectful

by placing 'god' in lower case letters-

It's not a proper noun, like, say, Yahweh

I think god is not too concerned with grammar

I think god is very fond of me

and allows me to chew on her bathrobe
like a puppy

We assign god gender

and human qualities so

it is easier to understand

We prefer god convenient and available

to help find parking in Ann Arbor and

cure cancer

yet there is greater godness whose Name

is beyond our comprehension

There are many Paths to the Heart of the Beloved

We all get there

Sometimes

Sometimes we are angels
cinched to the hip of God

What if we are
inseparable Oneness-with-God
temporarily embodied
as if in tight fitting shoes
This life

Sometimes we are needy humans and
god takes us out for ice cream

Chapel

In the quiet of chapel

fifty years ago

A stone loft, old oak

lingering incense clinging to heights, enveloping

An image of Sacred

A Moment

May we find 'holy place' and 'holy moment'

Towardness

Dear God
I see a picket fence
a country cottage, gardens

Each day a step
subtle, as if 'towardness'
Small doses of bravery
Crack open the door
just a smidge
That we may be Light

Ineffability

Dear God

I come into You

uncluttered of symbol and language

Not of form but *awakeness*

unhurried

Staying awhile

where time is not

Shedding adjectives

bowing to ineffability

and Presence

Happiness

Happiness comes up my driveway
Unsure of her intention, I hide
as if she's pushing religion with
those pamphlets and a clean shirt
Risky business
I mask up and wrestle her to the ground
She touches my cheek like the kiss of a child
Helpless, I surrender

Thin

Dear God
Your Dwelling so near
Some partially enter
unsure, feeling, testing
Some bump it as if a steel curtain
as if driving a tank
God sighs

The veil between us and God
is thinner than truck-stop toilet paper

Theologizing

God so loves

and makes a unique universe for each of us

with its own 'rules', circumstances

and perspective

It is difficult to live in community

A blessing and a curse, it is said

Some contend their own universe is the 'right' and 'only' way

Not helpful

Slow-walk among the forgiving purple flowers on the forest floor

Shards

Threads of our fabric

tiny tick-tack-toe shapes

intertwined, layered

space between, big enough for

a logging truck

a teeny tiny truck, driven by a

teeny tiny driver on a tiny road

Unless there are no roads, then she will fly

on tiny wings, the bucked logs chained firmly

on the way to a sawmill beyond the star

Any star will do, a tiny one, not out there but

in here, deep, deep in heart, making heat, sending light

enough

to light many worlds

Shards of God

VII
WISDOM, PRESENCE, GRATITUDE

Imprinted

Dear God

The sun does not wait in its travel

regardless our intent

Time, the great tease

passes and we are imprinted

in ways we did not suppose

Only in retrospect do we see

Only in stillness do

we know

Wiggling

Dear God

I can't find you

Am I hiding?

Under the couch?

In the belly of a whale?

How far must I go to escape you?

'I will hound you all your days' You say

'How can I forget thee' You say

'For you are held, and tattooed

on the palm of My hand'

Quit wiggling

Be Held

Washed

Dear God
Why this restlessness
as if sitting on the nose
of an endless freight train
trying to peddle it as if a bicycle
trying to make it go

Who cares
Step off
Rest at edge of Shady Pool
Soak feet in Holy Water
Be Washed

Constantly

Let each do her job
As if orderliness abides
As if goodness a possibility

As if Song amidst discord
As if She whispers your name
Constantly, endlessly

Minus 3

Cold out, minus 3

Exhale

Be blessed with gratitude

for no reason

Un earned

Un bought

Featherlight

Neither body nor thought

Unencumbered

Lofted in Current

Loosed from tight fitting shoes

just for a while

Receive Gift

Be Gift

Day Begins

Sun trying to penetrate morning chill

I bet on sun

I bet the chicken crosses road

I bet the goat stands on picnic table

and leaves an offering

Day begins

What did you expect

Fresh donuts?

Get up!

Make something happen

Brother Ass

St. Francis of Assisi, when old and crippled referred
to his body as 'Brother Ass'

Some of us are experiencing 'oldness' of body

Bodies like a barn-find '57 Buick Roadmaster

Clunky, not sleek like young live-forever bodies

In need of repair, parts hard to come by

Yes, we do drone on about our sputtering engines
and wobbling joints

It's not as if we can step out and climb into a new F-150

Wouldn't want to

At best we dwell in Wonderment

the breeze of God, just enough to move our wind chime

Formless

Into the formless heart of hearts

The quiet placeless place

The reign without reign

Only Presence

Rest in God

Go often, be refreshed

Made anew

Shimmering

God sometimes enters like a sliver

An unexpected harsh intrusion

We probe the entry with

our clumsy pocketknife

The wound heals over

leaving remnants

which resurface

shimmering

throughout a lifetime

Happiness (part 2)

Happiness,

the sister of Gratitude,

like a summer fog on the wetlands

envelops

Available

like her brother Presence

Let her lay upon you

pricking those dense defenses

Quit swatting her as if a mosquito

Four Fragments

Before I made you in the womb, I know you.
Jeremiah

Get off your ass.   Make something happen.
C.E. Hines (my dad)

Two prayers – Help me. Help me. Help me. (and)
Thank you. Thank you. Thank you.
Anne Lamott

Yahweh asks only this, to act justly, to love tenderly
and to walk humbly with your God.
Micah

Letters to God

A rickety platform

A Kool-Aid stand

on sawhorses in the yard

Kool-Aid, 3 cents

Few passers by

Ice cubes near melted

Mom's sugar settling to bottom

A sweet venture

A path with heart

Good try

Enough for now dear friends, the basket near empty

My bride and I noted our fiftieth wedding anniversary

yesterday, August 18, 2022

We went early for a bite at the tavern

Then walked to the ice cream place

Amidst the noise

May we Seek

May we be Sought

May we walk Kindly

Th

PART TWO
FRIDAY Rx

I
LONGING

Sadness

We all have a sadness

sometimes

sitting on us like an elephant

Even during sunshine

it catches up with us in all our pretty occupations

clinging to us like sand burrs

just for a while or sometimes longer

Relief

At the rest stop on the expressway

Great relief upon entering the men's room and seeing a urinal

Not the usual relief

But verification I've not entered the lady's room.

Battery

We charge the battery of our phone

And the battery of the dump trailer

And the sun charges the battery of the golf cart

And the sun charges the battery of each tomato

We rest in sleep charging our own batteries

Eight hours. Beep, beep, full! Up and run.

Endless cycles like an ox at the water wheel

Do we know how foolish we are, sometimes

the ends we'll seek to hide from

That Which Is

(or whatever Her Current Name)

Lunch

We have a longing

to enter the inner place

without sound or gravity

or image or symbol

or expectation or measure

and quiet the soul

snipping away grasping tentacles

Into free fall

(or is it soaring)

Into the limitless mindless mind

this nourishment

a light lunch with God

Lawn

Waiting on the lawn

outside of heaven

Having a coffee

Not enough of the old energy to sally forth

Not giving up, just resting

Biding time, as they say

Just beyond the fence

goodness aplenty

Actually not too bad right here, on the grass

cool breeze, shade

Pouch

Little pieces of hurt

kept in a pouch

A troublesome wart in the pocket of life

Toss it in the air

like a tennis ball

Hit it like those TV tennis champs

Boink!

Past the moon

Shattered

into weightlessness

Driveway

Let me walk the driveway

And meet the morning sun

Let me be small –

Small enough to greet the gray green tree frog

Unhurried

chipmunks chattering

Wild berries at rest

What to make of the day?

Maybe step lightly

and leave it alone

Temple

Oh temple of the soul

blundering bumper of walls at night

attached for a lifetime

Brother Ass

stimulated by a mere five senses

a toothache for eighty years

this body a tight fitting pair of shoes

      Persevere

find a tiny lens

a cloudy eye into the heart of God

Ponder

It is prayer

to sit and ponder

reinventing creation each morning

while the dog laps water

from the toilet

and the radio drones an ache of continents far

    Stars clear in the sky

        a sharp slice of the moon

resting

        in the vest pocket of God

Out

Unable to welcome light
Heart propped with withering posts and
temporary signs of 'keep out'
Too dark

Beauty
cloaked in negativity
Hardly a chance for her,
or her sister,
Wisdom,
to make an appearance
Both like fragile eggs in the pocket of a dirty apron
waiting patiently
for release
like seasoning sprinkled on creation

Whisper

Starved for a God moment-

just the slightest tickle

a miracle in a thimble

Whisper my name

Yeah, me, Your loyal lap dog

begging a morsel

Not my best Buddha self

needy and craving

    Make the day into night, move the planets left and right

Make the tree frog hide in view

Any ol' thing will do

    I am here, just in case, here I am

Grace

Sometimes we live in the dark for so long
that we forget the light
Everyone's had moments of light
haven't they –
when Presence is close and overwhelming
and we want it to stay forever?
Some try to possess it
inventing handles
Some think it is
result of chemicals or spicy ethnic food
Some call it Grace
a piece of precious we cannot hold
and yet remains, as if in our cells

Morning Damp

Open the glass

Let in the morning damp

Birds tentative

Chipmunks with muddy boots

Air pressure expanding and contracting, ears popping

Each leaf dripping

Night water seeping between blades of grass

through loam as if making earth coffee

between stones and grains of sand deeper
and deeper into the aquifer

sifting, purifying

Each drop of water a tear from God

longing for home

Wind

Our cares and attachments
weigh us down and
change the gift of color from radiant to dull

We are seekers while young
Then householders
Perhaps the onset of wisdom finds us
while raking leaves in the wind
The laughing swirling wind
slave to no concern
unraveling our tidy plans

Flow

As if we could see – and paint life
as if with watercolors on flat canvas
A snapshot
foam on beer, condensation on frosty glass
a pretty maiden, flower in hair
a smile
a moment
one among many – add color and dimension
and time, forward and back
atoms and molecules
universes known and unknown
we begin to experience complexity
Is it ours to build further?
Or to be of heart in the moment we have?

II
ALONG THE WAY

Gift

The gift of existence – the beating heart we cuss

as over-subscribed, broken and put upon by the fates

For a morning minute

be still and mystified

soften mouth and jaw

push back fear

move into day

with kindness

and intention

Her Face

My brother took out money

for the person with the sign by the side of the road

Embarrassed, I wouldn't look in her face

She'd spend the money on … something

      She doesn't like being there, he tells me,

reaching across, forcing me the bill as the light turns green

impatient drivers behind as I pass money

real human eyes burning for a moment

mine, hers, sparks of compassion, his

as we move on

window closed

Box Store Girl

Box store Corporate Miscreants
I've been wronged! Mislead!
I'll stew till my ears steam
I'll go back and yell at the girl

The one who got out of bed and fed her three-year-old and
took her to her mom's and drove to work in that old car
the one that needs brakes
to her paltry wage job and
her helpful silly vest with her name
She'll be waiting, calling me 'Sir'

I see her
slightly haggard, a notch shy of pretty, trying her best –
beautiful beyond comprehension
I can't be mean to her –
really, impossible

Old Fellows (circa 1995)

Implement at road side, for sale

Dad and I park the truck and walk up

I stand on the farmhouse porch as my aging father

bangs the door harder than necessary

An equally ancient man, roused from nap opens the door

glasses and hair askew, suspenders pulled over stained long johns

large belt buckle hanging loose

      The two stare, wordless

sizing each other as if old gun slingers

I step back, uncomfortable, slightly embarrassed

at this toothless encounter, this pending chesty negotiation

      Finally, my dad,

 "What outfit you with?"

"Old China Marines. You?"

"Fleet Marines, detached"

I notice the old man's belt buckle emblem, and melt further away

as they each recite serial numbers and landings

from a lifetime ago in the Pacific of WWII

I was not part of this conversation

a fellowship beyond my comprehension

Jelly

Sticky jelly on the light switch – Grandchildren

Pleasant thoughts

Rapidly passing years

Innocence and wonder

A wash of color, a palate of infinite possibility

Rosy cheeks glisten like stars

As it should be

All of this

even though its likely my own jelly on the switch

Drummer

I see the drummer behind the band

He lost a young son

I wrote to him a note

Maybe as much for me

I know him only a little and now this other kinship

I explain how at the grocery store in the
fresh vegetable section

it finds you and

hits you in the chest, out of nowhere

stinging, taking your breath away

Let it wash over you, I tell him, don't hurry
or hide from it, let it run its course

than fold it like a handkerchief and set it aside

I don't remember exactly what I wrote

It might have been too invasive

I did not hear back

And now two years later after the park concert he
loads his drums

and walks in shadowy summer dusk

I greet him, Hey

He nods, Thanks for the note, he says

Raggedy

These must be the raggedy underwear she mentioned

Shall I toss them now

or wear one last time?

If the garbage collector finds them, need they be fresh and clean

or, if I get in a wreck today, the nurse at emergency

you know?

Shall I risk?

Pretty comfortable

I'll toss them after wearing

one last time

If I remember

St. Pat's Day in North Carolina

A blessing

May you eat spaghetti like a small child

May the meatball find you

May you walk sunny paths on quiet morns

May that awful fear come not to be

May your time at airports be short, your landings soft

May the smile of children penetrate your soul

May your needs be few, your wants dissolve

May you fly, effortlessly, blissfully,

on magic carpet with the Beloved

even though most of the time you are sure it's bullshit

May your day be mixed in the breath of God

For surely *that* you are

Holy Day

Fourth Wednesday of the month

government funds magically into my account

What to make of this

free money suddenly appearing

Almost embarrassing

Yes, I worked for it, made deposits, waited

I hear of those in need

but don't send the money back

keeping it instead in a little pile to buy gasoline or take my wife to dinner

She still works at a job where she gets paid

I still work, too, at various jobs but don't get paid, except by the government

Here, let me take a moment to check the computerized direct deposit …

Yup, there it is, like manna for the Israelites

Maybe I can buy something new and shiny, a bell for my bike or new baskets

from Shaefer Hardware downtown, with the squeaky wooden floors, where my dad took me in the fifties.

If we were lucky, we'd enter the ancient elevator and ascend by pulling a heavy rope

up to a secret haven full of dusty treasure

I wish we could go back there

the bell on my bicycle just not the same

'wing, wing'

Firewood

So much wood to split

and then to stack

in long neat piles two rows deep

loose enough for a mouse to run through

but not the cat chasing it

Piles covered to shed water and hold snow

sides exposed for drying

Long rows like bank accounts assuring winter warmth

Ash and cherry, oak and hickory, a little elm and hornbeam

each piece handled five times

finally settling among glowing coals

thoughtfully and efficiently

radiating warmth

More cumbersome than the snake-like quiet of natural gas

Tactile

Makes you feel alive

And ready for a nap

Up North

Young boy holding a large turtle

in his lap like a cat

How *does* one snuggle with a reptile

Young boy with shovel and ax

digging and chopping

as if it makes a difference

(It does)

Young girl with a frog

large green and wet

nose to nose whispering

Children like a mob of fish

all in unison sprinting to a next adventure

At dusk flaming torches on sticks

crushed between graham crackers

with chocolate.

Ticks enough for a zombie movie

Ten children power washed and clean

Off to bed

Half an hour after me

Green Apples

Boy, about eight, sitting on the toilet after eating green apples,

terrible stomachache

Same guy, 60 years later, waking four A.M. identifying with, and *being* that little person, living that moment, now

The old guy and the boy are the same- the *time*, as we say, is the same, indistinguishable

I am the young boy and the old man right now, housed in this flexible body suit

pretending to be lineal, stretched like bubble gum, for a lifetime

With a certain orderliness

we act our age

the body suit no longer drawn to green wormy apples.

Egg

Young girl

afraid of spiders, ticks, and

things creepy crawly

spots an egg in the dusky shadow of the hen house

Chickens clucking near, she

musters all her bravery and steps onto straw
and droppings

reaching

extending fully, she grasps a warm brown egg –
a jewel for her dad

She smiles

He smiles too

A fine victory

Barefoot Waterski

Almost light at almost six

Meet at the dock, expensive inboard,

Detroit V-8 sitting lustily center-boat, a throaty rumble idling across glassy surface

Colorful suits, in the water now, bare feet, "Hit it!" and the engine roar

Up and gliding at the end of a long rope

giant rooster tails from our heels at thirty-eight miles per hour

glistening in the rising sun visible clear across the lake

not so long ago

pastime in past time

Away

San Juan Islands –
Like the chilly craggy coast of Scotland
and the sea goes on forever
while giant cedars and firs
stand like arrowheads
pointed at God

History compresses on vacation
Sounds and sights blend
As if in a mixing bowl
How are your legs today and feet
It's good to be away
In the swirl
And to go home

Grandchildren

Driving for grandchildren

8:15, pick them up

To the bakery, an apple fritter please

and to the tractor place, stop and

climb mighty land crawlers

Quarter mil a pop? No problem

I'll take four

Then home. Nana hugs. Dog hugs. Dig a carrot.

Climb a tree. Drive the cart.

Haul some wood. Swim the pond. Whoo!

Need a nap. Not yet noon. Day and a half to go.

Two days a week not needing to know or judge

Two days without the gnawing ache of managing the universe

Juxtaposition

Dawn a drizzle, earth all green at rest

Modern robot in the kitchen noisily harvesting ice cubes, readying for human consumption

An odd enterprise and juxtaposition:

the work of Mother Gaia and that of Brother Man

proud lime-green bathtubs and leisure suits

avocado wall panels in the family room

and prized stereo speakers,
large as washing machines

filled with woofers and tweeters

but none so glorious as the wren singing
out my window

in the shifting hazy green of morning's misty leaking blue of sky and promise of day

Fall

Glass door closed, fall's first cool

Dog's toenails on hardwood

Wife prepares to teach

Festival soon, field mowing in earnest

Other work continues, harvesting, preparing for market

Always something needs the oil changed

My own oil is overdue

maybe a little STP would help the knees

Green leaves of the canopy at rest

waiting patiently for sun

Dust of the road not yet stirred

Oak

Giant grandfather oak vertically split, leaning across the driveway

tired of holding on, weeping to the west

We took her down, safely

An old friend, a timber cutter

A slot here, a wedge there, the long-bar Stihl fully plunged

A mighty crack, a moment of rush, thunder heard half mile away

as the tree fell after countless decades

humbly, to lend warmth many cold nights

Timothy (2016)

"Hi Beautiful," he says, too loud, his arms spread, his silver hat-hair wild as he greets the hostess. She is beautiful and takes in stride his greeting as she leads us to a table. I'd picked my brother up at the group home to go to breakfast.

"That's not appropriate," I say.

"You're not my dad," he says.

She is indeed beautiful.

It pisses me off. He orders inefficiently, a la carte breakfast, this and that on the side, expensive tomato juice. "Order off the menu," I grumble. (Who drinks tomato juice?) He shares his side of bacon with me and offers sausage links for my dog.

He'd lost the debit card I got for him. The family joke was: His drug dealer doesn't take Visa. I couldn't give him cash. He'd bum money on the street. A guy gave him a hundred dollars couple days ago, five twenties. "How much you got left," I ask, sipping coffee, finishing breakfast. One twenty, four ones. I noticed he had change for the parking meter. "Where's the rest?" I ask. He gave twenty to such and such, a pack of smokes to so and so …

He was a crazy artist, a semi-street-person, giving away his art to coffee shop servers, generous to a fault, unaware, unfiltered, unconcerned with propriety. He saw the innocent wonder of the beautiful young woman at the restaurant and did not fail to celebrate that moment.

He was difficult.

He died a couple days later. Tipped over and died at the group home. "Drop me off here," he'd said, "by the bus station." "I love you," he said. "Okay, yeah," I said, "see you later."

I shake my head in wonder.

The Day

Perhaps today is the Day

when the sky opens- a crystal glow

and all accessories of earth

melt like Styrofoam battle tanks

arithmetic fails

time relents

And God reaches out His mighty arms

(He has arms today)

And He says to me Greetings, you in whom I delight

It occurs to me that God is rather formal

And He says Behold, Let's get outta here

And I am happy climbing deeper into Her mighty kangaroo pouch of being

                I'll give it till noon

If it doesn't happen

I'll drive to Kluck's in Ypsi

for chili dogs

Wonderful

Check messages

See if anyone says you are wonderful

Like eating popcorn or chewing gum –

we check the machine

Curious addiction

Can't we know we are wonderful?

Please:

you are perfection like a tasty tart apple-

wonderful!

Acorns

Acorns letting go like little skydivers

Plink plinking on the roof and deck

Little ball bearings of delight

Parachutes unopened

A one-way trip

to deer and squirrels in queue for feasting

    Like turtle eggs

some few hatch into new life

One acorn in a googol turns into a giant oak

arms spread like a mighty grandpa

connecting sky and earth

Career

When I had work for the men

they were happy

It was my part to get good work

non-adversarial

Do the job

collect the pay, move on

A good journey mostly

Always evolving

constant focus or get crushed

At some point get out of the way

You can't just stay out of habit, you get hit by a bus

and spill your purse in the street

Hummingbird

Hummingbird scolds as I pee off the porch

Her nectar near my ear this foggy morn

Who *is* the porch boss?

Each of us confused

going about our business

now retreating

thinking, reasoning,

to the extent that humans and bumblebee sized birds think and reason

We could set a schedule of mutually agreed times and needs

or

I could pee elsewhere

Grandma Gail

Grandma Gail died after a hundred years

I hear her voice and tone, enunciation and vocabulary

in her sons, delightfully so in Bill, the horseshoer

I'd asked son Bob if he'd given her permission to let go

He pondered the question as we sat by fire sipping beer

Son Woody plotted a family cemetery, it took a while

they're not a fast family

Maybe they were stalling and she knew it

Making her wait

At last complete, a pleasant location
in well-drained gravel

A fine place to rest

after all the heavy lifting

Side Altar

At my father's funeral I told the priest

he'd been angry at the Church for half-a-century

having to be married at the side altar

because he was Lutheran

My mother Catholic

in 1946

As if he were some kind of second-rate human

      Was he able to get past those feelings, asked the priest

Sure, I said,

A couple days ago

Christmas 1952

Laying on my father's chest

squishing his pack of Camels

and wanting a bike for Christmas

A red one I said

as he lifted me in the air

suggesting a chocolate color bike

Chocolate would be fine, I agreed

which was the color of the

Huffy Convertible bicycle near the tree

the following morning

I must have just turned four

                    Oh, for each of us a fond memory

a complex father

like gravity tilting our being

Subscribe

We don't get to choose our neighbors

or the spouses of our children

We don't get to choose our parents or siblings

Unless we subscribe, as some do, to the notion that we set this up in advance, prior to birth, our lifetime a theatre of sorts where we play it out, go back, trade roles and do it again, ten or a hundred times. All this in an instant, simultaneously, a moment of trial separation from God, frequently hellish, as separation from love is.

Is that how it is?

Beats me

Kiss

Laying on the couch reading

Granddaughter, age 3, approaches

"Grandpa, I wanta kiss you"

I lean my cheek toward her and receive a glob of sticky goo on my face

Back to reading

"Grandpa, I wanta kiss you"

Cheek extended a second time

"No Grandpa, I want a tissue!"

Rubbing

Tall oak, twelve inches in diameter, straight up

nine feet from where I sit

rubbing the house when the wind blows

It would have been easy to cut the oak prior to building except

I don't cut living oak

Which shall I amend: The house or the oak?

Is there a middle ground

a non-destructive coexistence?

I'd hate to chop down my house

Perhaps if I stay out of it

the house and tree will co-mingle and

birth baby tree houses

Stone Wall

Who commissioned this work of art

This rambling curved stone wall that is our life

Tended by many hands

Shifting around trees and forest

Indirect at best

And weathered smooth

Moss covered here and there

Who said enough material exists

And so what if deer jump its height

And mice burrow below

Bacon

Early morning

Sitting at restaurant with grandson, age 4

Waitress brings each of us a plate

Pancakes, scrambled eggs, bacon

Grandson ignores his food, takes a piece of bacon from my plate and eats it

I sip coffee, watching.

He takes second piece of bacon from my plate, eats it

"What are you doing?" I ask

"Grandpa, I'm sharing with you."

Growing Pains

We can't dip our children in a pool of protection
as if in hot fudge or an industrial coating
They must paddle their own canoe
bumping rocks and getting sunburned
even though we warn them
too many times
We want seat belts and lead free paint
but kids have to be loosed or else
suffocate in a whitebread cocoon
They have to get skinned legs and risk poison ivy
if they are going eat lush berries near the path

Apologies to William

Shakespeare remains difficult

Out, damned spot!

Trips to Canada, the stage in England

Cliff's Notes and frustrated instructors

Sure, something's there but …

So much to grasp

neither can I play violin nor

drink good Bourbon without Coke

Each takes time and investment of heart

I prefer to amble a sunny edge of wetland

with grandchildren discovering blackberries and wildflowers,

mushrooms the size of Narnia, and

green turtles big as John Deere tractors

Summer 1959

Oh, we could run forever in summer evening play

Tackle pom-pom, hide-and-seek

Impossibly thin bodies, dirty with ripped shirts

Unconcerned, unsupervised

All the fun we could have between supper and dark

Little kids too, allowed to join, teased, pushed down and picked up –

everyone could play, the rules vague and fluid,
between sprints to bases-   a hut, a hole,
a chicken coop

till we came in and bathed the earth from our bodies

and soundly slept

Weld

In the shop welding a brush cutter

needed right away at the farm

Super-hot electricity melting steel together

Reinforced with additional metal

without having to mine the earth and experiment for

a thousand years

Thank you, old timers, for trials and failures

burned eyes, calloused fingers, hammers and anvils

that I might simply walk to the shop

flick a switch and meld molten metal hot like the sun

Disproportional, this bounty

Memorial

All these people

all those times

pictures, youthful carefree moments

pinned to the waving wall of a yard tent

and us, now, bending forward like old people

Campfire singeing the edge of ragged emotion

Junk emptied from the barn, a lifetime of worn stuff

ready for discard

loaded on a two-axle trailer by sons and beer-laden buddies

Just bend over and do the work

sweat it out like a pesky cold

Later, exhausted by well-meant hugs see

children run carefree chasing a large ball

sunshine, the yard green and shaded as

healing flows into crevices and seeps in

Columbine

Columbine, the flower, tall and purple
sneaking outside the safety of large stones
at garden's edge
into crushed gravel and danger of driveway
How dare they?
Fragile beauty
moving at will
unbound by rules-
borders, territoriality

The children encircle with stones the curious columbine,
rerouting large automobiles
protecting innocence, as children will

Carrot

First carrot of the year

with grandson

Like an orange Creamsicle

from childhood

only better

Or an Orange Crush

from the machine at the gas station

where your dad put in a dime and slid the bottle along the chilly rack

once in a while

and now

this orange carrot, with wild green hair, at the farm with grandson

Back Home

Fireflies gather at dusk

Welcome home tired Old Guy

Familiar driveway weaving between walnut and oak

around hill past two tree huts and the shop

grass sneaking between pieces of crushed granite

car swallowed by garage

Rabbits and chipmunks scurry from lurking Driveway Cat

Darkness wraps and bundles Homestead as if a package

to be sent into Night for rest and healing

then seized by Tomorrow

another Dawn

Going Back

Sister on her way to work

in morning dark

a first day back after her spouse died

Sitting here unable to assist her

Sending beams of encouragement

like the parent of a first day kindergartener

fragile like tinkling china cups

exposed to chilly winds

that seep through walls

High School Wrestling

Underwood the Hulk

was written on the picture

of a strongman taped to a home team locker

at the Christmas tournament in 1964

a two day event, the first for me

We second-string wrestlers wearing old uniforms were entered along with the varsity

Locker rooms were quickly trashed and disgusting after weigh-in

Still, no one dare rip down the menacing figure of Underwood the Hulk

I spied him at his locker with his big chest and Buddy Holly glasses

The following morning, we met in the semi-finals

It is not so much the match that I recall, as the hour before, under the bleachers

frightened to a point of breathlessness, for the first time unknowingly maneuvering into an altered state

a hyper mindset, not to win (never really a consideration) but, *not to chicken out*,

to be, somehow, *totally present*

Later, that evening, after our varsity guy wrestled for third place, I lost in the championship match

not yet understanding the art of mental preparation –

a path I'd stumbled onto that morning under the bleachers prior to soundly defeating

Underwood the Hulk

Brownies

Lunch table next door at the organic farm

A half dozen farmers and interns, bounteous fresh produce

I brought brownies

"Who made the brownies?" an intern asked

"A friend of mine," I said, "a peace activist"

"Oh," he said, reaching for the plate

A young woman, vegan, new to the group leaned forward

"She's a poet and teaches at prison," I said

The young woman's cheeks gained color

I paused, watching her focus intensify

"She went to Africa to hold sick babies," I said

The young woman's chair slid back as she reached across the table

"Maybe I'll try one of these," she said

Parts

Our father's work bench

A glass tray of parts

from a forgotten project

A film of dust and oil

Perhaps a carburetor or the motor of a machine

Brittle glasses from the dime store

Needle nose pliers, tiny screwdriver

What to do with memories

And jobs incomplete

Is lifetime ever complete

Does it reverberate, tiny tickling vibrations

ever here ever now

Travel

Early morning London

walking by a disheveled beggar

It's like driving by a vegetable stand on the highway –

you go by a few times

I should stop

after Starbucks where I'll spend

several British pounds on coffee

then study strange coins

while the ill-kempt blanket-clad street person exhales

cigarette smoke into frosty air

acting his part

waiting

as I drink expensive coffee

Buddy

My best buddy of eighth grade died recently

I was displeased with him-

his lack of restraint

taking the easy way instead of working

toward his boundless potential

He moved out of state

after retirement from the factory he hated

where he abused substances for decades

somehow avoiding dismissal

I didn't know that, late in life, he'd come clean

and helped others struggling with abuse

These later years

all my unnecessary judgments and displeasure

Voice

In the field where we played baseball every day

lay loose pipe end to end, each twenty feet long

A hundred of them

To be buried and change our childhood paradise

into a subdivision

Inside a pipe midfield I spied a one-inch ball-bearing

halfway from either end

Being ten at the time, and alone, it seemed a good idea to shimmy in

and retrieve the hidden gem

I got all the way to the ball-bearing before realizing I was stuck

unable to go forward or back

Awareness and panic set in

Then a Voice, not my own child's voice, but mature adult-like, masculine as I recall,

comforting and with surety,

came from within me or from outside, I am not sure of where, but clearly voice

words instructing, "Relax. Back out."

Which, after making myself small, I did

I didn't think much of it at the time

An angel perhaps? Every night we said the prayer "Angel of God, my guardian dear,

to whom God's love commits me here …"

And now, six decades later, with grandchildren that age, I have frightening flashbacks

and fear for them

And still gratitude and awe

for the Voice

New Glasses

I ordered new glasses

They arrived crooked

The salesperson studied my face

The receptionist behind the counter suggested

my ears were crooked –

the glasses were fine

I asked if maybe she had other things she could focus on

She said, no really, we get crooked, especially as we age

different parts of the body change size and move around

I didn't ask for examples

but continued to view my slightly unbalanced ears –

brackets for vision hardware

I could better see both women

Nice smiles, pleasant, fairly balanced

Someone's Daughter

Chilly young woman

looking as if she slept on the street

inhales deeply on her cigarette

in early morning frosty air outside a coffee shop in south Wales

Purple highlights in her hair, tattoos, bangles

Two more drags on the smoke

before dousing it on a patio table

Cautiously she enters the stylish coffee shop, eyeing the busy baristas

and glides by to the tiny unisex restroom

After a while she reemerges, again looking toward the workers

She exits the store

and relights her smoke

III
CALLING OUT GOD

Out of Order

The knocker on God's door must be out of order

Surely God would answer if only God knew my concerns

I want to tattle on creation for being unfair

For taunting

The yoke oughtn't be loaded on those already burdened

Open up!

I insist God send down little angelic load adjusters

      Surely righteousness prevails

but in the dark night it is difficult

at the edge of understanding

on the doorstep of God

Prayer

The childhood prayer

we learned from our mom –

Has its term expired

like the vaccination on our arm?

Is there a new prayer more hip and timely

fitting changing fashion

more inclusive

less fearful of spooky forces?

Shall we pray in colors and silence

in thunder, lightning and supplication

in song and dance

in the void without image

on easel with brush and bursting shapes?

      Any way at all will do

ask your mom

Embrace Goodness

I keep trying to figure

as if it's my job to manage creation
It never happens the way we think –
Perhaps life just goes on and we live it
Sometimes it works and sometimes we take lumps
      Still
I wait for the great burst of light –
the heroic resolution when
we rest unburdened in the arms of the Beloved
      Meantime
sit near moving water when you can
Embrace goodness
Release anger and hurt
Love a child and learn from her or him
Till soil
Welcome wildlife
Slow down
and at eventide engage the farthest star
as if it were in your lap
for surely it is

Forgiveness

Forgiveness

What if we acted the fool

and could wake in the morning

and erase it all?

Some would return to folly out of habit

or boredom

What if we could really forgive ourselves

and others?

        Could I forget thee?   Let tongue cleave to palate should I forget thee

Like dribbling water wearing down stone

the call

Come back to me, come back to me

Holy Visit

I need a Visit –

just for a moment

to realign the pick-up-sticks

all jumbled

Could'ya stop by

Hound of Heaven

Any Name

The slightest sign always enough

Oh?

I need to be quiet and listen better, blah, blah, blah

Come on, just a little jolt, a mini fix

Humor me, your faithful compadre, blah, blah

Sunlight

Friends, clean socks

Sure, sure

Enough already?

Ok, tell you what, give you another chance

I'll be here

Look me up

Lifted

Little boys and girls

let out for the summer

trying on the illusion of separation

wearing costumes of individuality

Look at me!

I'm a clown! I'm a hero!

Yes, beautiful

though slightly dissatisfied

Lift us up! (we implore)

and sometimes

we are

Lifted

Early Morning Grouch

Squirrels and birds on the porch

Green in the canopy, wakeful moon of last night

Coffee trying to penetrate the grime, trying to locate a pocket of hope

New dock sinking in the mud

Dozens of chipmunks scurrying in the yard, fearless, as if I'm not the mightiest of beings

as if their little boroughs are satisfactory protection

I'll get a cat

Not likely

The day will get better

I'll brew another cup

And split some wood and mow the lawn

And take a nap

Is that enough

Is there a check-off list

Be righteous, walk humbly with God, mow the lawn

Help

Let me help you fix your flat

Here by the side of the road

Obvious need

Just want to help a little bit

Just today

Can't heal the earth, the sadness

All that sadness

makes you want to hide

makes you want to cry out

Lord, Lord

Sleepless on the Western Slopes

Chainsaws and dead men
Invasive plants and invasive people
We're all invasive
on some level

Tears come and clean the debris of heart
Which bubble up as bad dreams
Breaking up sleep

Chipping away at the steep surface of mountain side
Neither climbing up nor sliding down
Only chipping chipping away

Yard

Land outside

cleansed of frightening predators

Only pleasant beings allowed, blue birds and wrens

Insistent mosquitoes separated by window screens

Frightening bears, driven off along with other indigenous dwellers

The corners clearly staked, except in the wetlands where no one wants to walk

Ownership written down in convoluted descriptions

and stored at the township hall where old people gather for mac and cheese

How come I get to have a little piece of Eden

sitting on the thin crust of a wiggling planet

in a warped solar system

in a spiraling universe

for this one blink of an eye

Woodchuck

Neither a vegetarian nor an excessive consumer of meat,

I consider shooting the woodchucks who have undermined the gardens

Rascally invaders

Is my garden and porch more important than their livelihood?

Wars are fought on such matters

I was relieved to read that Ramakrishna slapped mosquitos

or was it Gandhi?

Still, I am not sure of the enterprise

not wanting to further upset the spin of the planet

Megan and Jake

Day begins, a piece of clay to mold
Default to warm and safe and plenty

What to make of those adrift
bobbing in hopelessness
bald tires, heater broke
tools in disarray, no tools at all
no skills, not a clue
Get up! We say, Rise!

It goes deeper –
to the molecules of hurt

Maybe I'll go to dinner, or buy a new car – I'll
feel better

Or maybe, be a teacher
One who is kind, and teaches
patiently, with grace, over a lifetime

Omega, N.Y.

In the extended moment worthy disciplines combine

and unworthy ones slip away

The young woman with tattoos

scattered about her body like mosquito bites

perhaps in time the dots will connect

Her leap of faith so visual

Her mom worries,

"Why can't she just have babies,

after a big wedding, (which we can't afford) you know what I mean"

It's risky, *living*. Maybe we oughtn't have come breathing up from water

But since we have

we choose a path

not perfect at first

only gradually freeing of clutter –

toward a humbling scent, the very breath of God

Heroic Myth

Overwrought of heroic myth

Capes and glory

Youth permissioned to kill

Under the guise of service

Under a banner of nation, an unlimited ad campaign

and colorful swagger

young boys (and now girls) buy in

(less boring than community college)

But grown-ups?

We bring home a dead boy

and call him a hero, and say he sacrificed all

It never comes up, what a lie we told, that he bought into

All those cars lining the street at the funeral

It never comes up, that it wasn't such a good idea sending him away, techno-dressed, licensed to kill

Himself killed, by an equally beguiled youth

Paint

Takes a while for paint to dry

We put our fingers on the sky of dawn

mussing the colors –

we slip in bravely

flowing with intent

waiting for the moment-

Or – when the moment does not avail

inventing the moment

We are made in the image of God,
like God's shadow

or Her painted toenail

When We Were Younger

Those clothes we wore

That buckle on our shoes

Those songs we sung

Colors and concepts once clear

melted and blurred like a rained-on homecoming float

That smiling European Mary with child

the cool blue of her wrap

faded

        Seeds remain

the pendulum swings

new symbols emerge

some silly, some earnest

new coat-hooks upon which to hang

our yearning yearning hearts

Quandary

To be active in the world. Or to live in quiet seclusion

To be a worker at the crossroads. Or a silent holy person

To preach. Or whisper to a single soul

To know with certainty. Or to be often unsure

To have met Personal Savior. Or to Wait

To be about the work of God.   Or to wonder if much human activity misses the point.

To be right. Or to be kind

To fear and respect the mighty Godhead. Or have a good laugh with the Beloved

To list precepts and documents of faith. Or listen to the wren sing

To hold language and written word as static in meaning.   Or, In the beginning was Word and Word became flesh and dwelt among us

Tipping

Is there a tipping point –

the 'Big One'?

Has it to do with oil or water,

plate tectonics, government?

Is it likely to happen in our lifetime?

Will they say, Well, obviously

the signs were there

      Or

maybe –

a bluebird will fly into her rickety house

and a butterfly land on

an orange flower, and we will watch and

dissolve

into a pool of gratitude

Jump

We want good sounds and shiny objects

and smells and tastes to make us whole

I sit outdoors and the wren settles my heart

Am I able to have the same sensation sitting near the city dump in a nation of poverty?

Not likely

The dump, the wren and the green of the canopy are temporary and illusive

Pointers and symbols of mind seeking oneness with that which remains in shadow just beyond everyday comprehension

What is it like to 'jump out of our skin'
just for a moment

And see with clarity

Some

Some among us walk in shadow
as if in quicksand
as if in excess gravity, in pain
    And some among us step lively
naturally gifted, unaware
of those beaten down
    The gifted ones
who seem blessed
but are without compassion
carry a millstone
              of unknowing

Better

Feeling gloriously better after illness

The urge rises to proclaim gratitude to the deity

Thank you! Thank you

for this absence of misery, this healing

only days ago incapacitated

      Yet – shall we lend equal responsibility to the deity for illness?

It wasn't as if I got sloppy drunk and crashed in the gutter – I was innocent

this time

If we praise the good, shall we curse misfortune?

An old question

Bearded philosophers and theologians over millennia proclaim definitive answers

usually a bit wordy, while

I remain uncertain

yet filled of gratitude

Stick

A single crooked limb sticking up from the lawn

as if fallen from a larger tree

yet slightly alive and growing

Braced with a steel stake

bare and ugly all winter then suddenly

flowering, beautifully lushly bountifully filled beyond capacity

this same spindly stick

Can something be both beautiful and not beautiful?

Is beauty a fleeting moment?

Shall we cherish its brevity

shall we embrace and breathe in this sneeze of God?

When

When is the time to be whole

To set stuff aside

and *be*

We wait for seasons

and jobs to complete

for trinkets and fool's gold

Could we be a Zen short-order cook

with a paper hat

Could we become unimportant

and charitable

a chance meeting

a tiny needle piercing a heart of stone

Body

I'm about done with this body, said Uncle Bill
shortly before he died
What if our body is like 'a cold'
something we 'get' and then 'get over'?

What if God is not anthropomorphic –
not a 'He' and does not have arms?
You gonna be okay with that?

What if we are –
formless
yet, somehow there is
caring and *knowing*
of each blade of grass and the chirping of the smallest bird?

Altar

Early morning dark

in stillness waiting

A red glass hummingbird feeder

gathers light just before dawn

standing in for the ever-lit red candle

near the altar of a musky cathedral

The light is on

I see you

The Trek

I screw up so many times
I'd be lost without forgiveness
Is Forgiveness a 'stuff', like chocolate?

I don't think God keeps score
Keeping score is a human activity –
adding to the misery we insist on

Steer away from vexatious persons –
you don't change poison ivy by rubbing it
Still, respect its existence

It is not our job to be miserable
tread lightly, move on

Why

Why do some get to work at the hardware store
while others fall off the end of the world
Why do some have happy babies while others
suffer
Why do some have no idea at all
while others see clearly
Why do some struggle while
others are good at stuff

We don't get to know all there is to know
except in tiny sparks of understanding
once in a while
Tiny sparks that strip away our preposterousness
and leave us awestruck

Lauds and Vespers

'Help me Lord, Help me Lord'

Not a prayer, though said morning and night

not intentionally, but habitually, as if stepping onto a high wire

a humbling awareness

the delicacy of moment

the folly of presumed control

as if the ground is actually solid

Maybe it is a prayer

Tossed

The wind blows
Let me hook my lanyard to Your robe
and be tossed about –
needless
refreshed

Thank You for this life –
this one snowflake
this single brush stroke

IV
WIFE

Tea Cup

I almost put toenail clippings in my wife's tea cup

She wasn't home and was done with it

I would have dumped it and put it in the dishwasher

It was too cold to clip my toes out on the porch

the cup was there –

Yet –

Two score back

she was such a darling girl in college

It just didn't seem like the thing to do

She's still darling

Most of the time

Orphans by the Sink

I like it when she takes a green leaf

broken by the dog, and plants it

new, in a small jar at the window

and it grows into a plant

Little orphans by the sink, decades of them

And she will dance around the house

with a watering pot, at the oddest time, her coat on, leaving for work

upstairs downstairs her route of plants

Orchids and those flowers, blooming

whichever season

Who's to tell them different

Slip Off

If I slip off first

you may not want to stay here

All the maintenance, overhangs to paint, high as an eagle's nest

We're not rooted like oaks and hickories

If I'm gone, you may not want to clear the driveway

or bring in the wood

I just say it, getting it over with, the saying part

Then again, it might be fine, who needs paint

You can work the gardens

and have the kids out

And call the birds by name

and the dog, whatever name

and the shop, empty of me

Give Billy the machine, he'll plow the drive

Oops! Here I am again reinventing your life
in my image

Together

Time together

Grumbling and rumbling

Like five year olds, my turn, my turn

Topics territorial jurisdictional fictional

Visitors arriving in a few days

She, diligent

Me, less enthused

about bedding or

trips to Ikea

I'll buy beer, perhaps liquor

Maker's Mark is it?

She'll get fruit, way too much, spilling over into the basement fridge,

Hey, wait, who moved my beer …

The silly things we do, and say

While paddling this canoe, together

Be

Wife reading a flier from the mail-

Special deals, dreams fulfilled!

                        I stare at blank page

a crossword puzzle without clue or structure

Or perhaps

one clue only:

Be

                Draw a little stream and some sunshine

A dog if you like and a child

and that house

the one with the crooked chimney

Hold the child's hand

Go from there

Autumn Morning

Cool sunless morning
  canopy of leaves still
Wife blanketed for autumn warmth
  content with cup of tea and readings
  the glass door open just a bit
  wind chime, its pendulum moving slightly
as acorns plink the deck
Now a soft dong of the chime
  a whispered reminder to waken further-
to bend time and light with intention
      Give us a minute
One more cup of tea
One more breath of quiet

Wednesday

Wednesday

I woke in panic

thinking I forgot and missed remembrance of the day Sammy died

As if the day slipped by without acknowledgement

I no longer dread the date's approach

but witness it, stare at it as if a mighty freight train, but from a distance, an observer

I did not miss the date, a few days hence, the 19th, confirmed with wife, breaching the topic

Next Monday. Perhaps I'll take a ride, escape to … where?

Shall I call his brother? Or J? I don't know.

The first few years I tiptoed around the day, sidestepping, holding breath until it went away

Now I have gratitude, a day of remembrance, a celebration of heart, more like Easter than Good Friday. I don't know why.

This life, this illusive slip and swirl of time, this merest instant of form before exhalation to formlessness yes … Yes.

Famousness

If I were famous

people would try to get ahold of me

at 2:00 p.m. as I contemplate a nap

I would have to respond, since the person bothering me would also be famous

You have to respond to famous people

I have enough trouble responding to people I love

let alone bothersome famous acquaintances

So, thankfully I sit alone on Sunday enjoying the rain

not even the dog begging supper

I am fairly famous to my wife but she doesn't bother me during nap time

Anniversary 45

An album of Simon and Garfunkel

A candle

A poster for the wall, things

I could buy for you, uncomplicated

money scarce and

wet shoes in the winter

didn't stop me from trekking to your door

wherever it was, at your school, your dorm

And you'd drive to see me, too far

in too worn a car, too late at night, for coffee and an hour

That youthful blush

Just to see your face

Nesting

New flower garden along the sloped edge of the shop
All that work, border stones gathered and placed
and now it's cold and still bulbs to be planted
Yet she persists, 'amending soil'
amending my perception
inviting order and beauty
where I used to throw sawdust in the weeds

Communication

Many years ago our son got off the bus from kindergarten with an upset stomach

As we greeted him my wife felt the waist of his pants –

These are so tight it must hurt

I just bought new pants, can you be growing that fast? Let's get these off

Beneath his pants he had on four pair of underwear

We asked, Why do you have on four underwear

He replied, You said to put on clean ones every day

V
ON WRITING

Poems

Writing poems

Sending them down a smooth slot as if from a gumball machine

many colors and flavors

hitting the end of the trough and popping out
on to the floor

Once in a while there is a good line or pair of words

or a twinkle from the farthest star

Once in a while it seems to work

Bread

I want to write a poem

and send it out right away

like fresh baked bread

still warm, to a friend or several

It smells so good, and butter will melt so nicely

But mostly it is better to wait and let it cool,

lest I offend someone

with these thoughts- they are thoughts after all

not fresh bread. Symbols and images pointing futilely

unable to say what is intended, feverish brush strokes on what cannot be painted

So if the bread is sometimes not so grand, set it on the porch for the mice

That would be okay, a feast of sorts

Spilled Soup

A poem sat

leaking off the page like spilled soup

Ingredients bumping noisily

symbols unable to meld

so wanting to point with meaning

to tell great truths

Little pieces of gravel in the road, what words are

sometimes locking perfectly into place, puzzle pieces of creation

Sometimes flying in the air cracking our windshield when

hearts become thick and dense like giant stones

(No offence to giant stones

whose hearts are like springtime flowers

purple and white, breaking through a blanket of oak leaves

painting the forest floor with new and fragrant sweetness)

Words and Meaning

Words come

like slippery logs

down a watery sluice

into a foamy pond

floating like marshmallows on warm cocoa

      Then again

sometimes words have to be pried out

like rusty nails

and put in proper order

      And later

words take on new meaning

so how can we hope to convey?

Yet they come

new words at dawn

like marsh gas seeping under the door saying as best they can until they become new Babel heaping up at the base of the tower until the tower is no more and once again children romp and play atop the crumbling battlements of former meaning

Of One

An audience of one

suits me fine

      If only

you could hear sounds

sent shimmering

scooped with clumsy spoon

stirred like mud pies and dried in the sun

sent for you alone this moment this day

reminding you

of the beauty that you are

Veil

Have a sip of tea

Look at words

See if they catch you

for a moment on your busy waking morn

Always a veil,

like mosquito cloth

separating us from what is most telling

A ghost of meaning

ever present

just out of reach

January

Winter cold
Words like boulders
dense and graceless
trying to penetrate molasses heart
Rain in January melting dirty snow
into plentiful mud

Suddenly
new snow at dawn, pure, straight down
an inch blanket
insulating the fur of deer
resting in straw lined pockets of wetlands
each a cozy nest in the hand of Creation

15 February

Dear Readers of Friday Rx,

I've been sick this week with a winter cold and have not been able to properly prepare a Friday Rx. Hope to be back in the saddle next week. Thanks for your loyal readership. Th

Morning Quiet

As if in a warm pool

and words are wet and melt into many shapes

then formlessness

    Meaning begins to massage body

and body is part of meaning and word

    Space between molecules vast

and worlds and ages drive through the large spaces as if on a mighty expressway

    Then birds chirp and the dog wants breakfast

    and we reassemble new

        Again and again

Veni Creator

Come, teach words

Send imagery

upside-down, inside-out

opposites connecting effortlessly

making something out of nothing and nothing out of something

shedding and shredding muddled armor

fresh and new

ineffable

That!

Yes, please

send That

Awareness

There is a moment from time to time

when the window is open and words fly in like musical notes

We are not warned of their coming but must be vigilant

like a woman making bread

sensors ready for good news

a whispered warmth

to be plucked from the weedy garden of today

and placed fragrantly in an open jar

for those who chance to stop by

VI
AWARENESS

Desiderata

Six pair of mallards glide on the pond
   invisible propulsion
      glass-like water, a sunny spring day
Just the slightest miracle
Spring peepers chat in the wetlands
Garlic greens peek out of winter mulch
Cardboard sign at roadside
   large dripping words running sideways
      youthful lettering: DOG FOUND
The fifth grade band honks through Old MacDonald then
   impossibly
  performs
     Ode To Joy
If we do not weep in gratitude, we are not paying attention

Lost

Sometimes we stop paying attention and get lost

We miss

little successes

    little flashes of light

        little pieces of redemption

that break the toil of journey

    We have to look, maybe strike the flint

Sometimes we make it happen, sometimes it just happens

Loss

When we lose a loved one to death

it is neither good nor bad –

it *Is*

Circumstances and timeliness may be weighty

yet

anger and blame

is not in the long run healthy

If we embrace a loving God (by whatever name and precept)

it is unlikely this God picks off loved ones as sport

    There is presumption in attachment

a clawing self-imposed burden

(indifference too is burden)

    We don't get to know all there is to know

    We best find a middle way, like the young Siddhartha

    Or like Mary Oliver, we must love with our whole being

and we must release

Beams

To be honest

and breathe what the universe has

whispered on raindrops and beams of light

Ever changing, ever constant

Gentle as a glacier

melting holy water

dawning daily

sweet fragrance of creation

smiling that quixotic smile

  Strap on boots, wash face

saddle up, hold on

or let go

Towardness

Rising from dark night

clutter of mind

Old fights refought foolishness

Waken!

In quiet, send out good intention

Though, surely

one cannot make a pot of soup with good intention

Start somewhere

a simple prayer

a *towardness* of heart

a whispered 'yes'

From the bed or chair with its indentation of your round ass

stir all of creation

get on with the *Work*

Granddaughter on Her Second Birthday

In the months after her fathers death, I had a near-panic need to explain to my granddaughter (not yet two) that which is unexplainable. I wrote pages and pages, as if to keep her (and self) from falling off the precipice. Later I realized I was trying to gather what (I thought)her father would tell her over a lifetime. The following lines are a distillation of those pages, completed for her second birthday.

Delaney Jane

On the whole, it is best not to be miserable.
It is best not to lend misery to others.
Kindness is good.
If you cannot love, act as if you love.   Love may follow.
Negativity is a habit,
        a poor choice leading down the worm hole of lesser gods.
Be positive even when you are breathed on by fear and doubt.
Peddle your bicycle bravely through the minefield of community.
Do not be fooled by fashion.
If you choose to believe,
believe that you are loved and embraced
        beyond your ability to comprehend.

Clippings

As much as a fingernail clipping

is how much we know

living our obvious life, and

what if it's not really that way – time, density, vibration,

the urgency of it all

life as a concoction of changing imagery

Every so often a bump in the road loosens the bindings of illusion

Cables

The bonds we hold
Cables across a foggy crevasse
Cables thick and stout
enough to carry a full gondola
of smiling tourists
to the other side of emptiness
I miss my son this morning
just once in a while

A coming trip with little sons and daughters
remembers him

Goodness and lastingness –
are they really real
or made up
just for a while?

It's okay
typing black squiggles on a white plane
to soothe the burn of giant cable
squeezing my heart
once in a while.

Trees

Stopping in wonderment while walking the woods

Don't have to do all that *work stuff*

Really don't care to go back

Let younger men move the pianos

or go off to war as they insist on doing

much to the sad exhalation of wordless trees

each blessing us

forgiving our youthful stupidity, our elder hubris

ever forgiving

Attend

Shall we meditate while the dog begs for breakfast
Or while a child cries
A child is always crying

To what shall we attend
Shall we do great things
or weed the garden
A season for all they say
Good ol' they

For many, dimness lingers
compassion rises slowly and is dispersed slightly
as if from a salt shaker

Until
a shadow of awareness
a breath of kindness
working at this
our walk with the Beloved.

Compost

Hillside and trees swallow an old waterslide along U.S. 12

So also the earth will swallow us

Meanwhile

let us not be miserable

Let us embrace the good

Let us be the good

Let us look past the folly of judgment

for surely we've not adequate information

Let us pet dogs and spit-clean a just picked carrot

Let us love unrestrained

Surely the earth will swallow us

All that insistence, just not so important

compost, good compost

Moment

Once in a while

dust and sediment settle

vision clears

noise abates

and we are with ourselves

be-lone, in the enormity of it all

unafraid, in the massive womb of creation

content, as if we've set aside this troublesome project

for a moment

Communion

Table

Clean off the table

Make a new day

Dive through the waterfalls

leaving old garments behind

Shameless

the wren sings while dropping waste

What will you choose, the song

or the droppings?

Some

Some harvest tiny pockets of gold

daily, confident that treasure abounds

Some feel locked in a room without direction

or social grace

Some have beauty

subject to time and gravity

Some are spectators only

Hopefully we are more than crickets under the lawnmower

or rude lawnmower drivers

hopefully we steer around orange wildflowers and the occasional foraging mouse

Toll

Pointless to hurry the honey bee

Or rush the butterfly from milkweed

Or coax an oak to walk

Lend time her toll

Her constant shimmering genius

Her mischievous promptings

Her relentless mirage –

A fresh cut flower in your hair

Fleeting beauty

Beauty indeed

Fortune

Calamity stalks the morning calm

Fortune though remains

lining her nest

with light and sound

and feathers

shed on a bed of oak leaves

Layers of life

guarded by a lone insistent bird

piercing dawn

like a lighthouse beam

"I am home, I am home"

Before

Before you were in

your mother's womb I know you

I am the tricycle you ride

the air you breathe

and the song before music

I am the shifting wave of every atom

the density of mass

and cool drink on parched sand

I am with you always

I am who am and cherish you

Falls Away

Blindness falls away

like pieces of broken crockery

over time

allowing vision into a pool

and we feel ourselves drawn to the pool, and immerse

and we are *of it*, and separation disappears

At first glance the pool is small and inviting

We want a taste

As we approach we realize the pool is enormous, and all consuming

We retreat many times

It's okay

No hurry

Clinkers

Like clinkers beneath a fire grate
stuff shakes out of us
a bit at a time

Enlightenment, Resurrection,
Awakening

Not frequently realized
A lot of tributaries to explore
We all get there eventually
Many paths

Traps

We invent traps

while laying in bed

then jump into them

'This is terrible' we say

'all this stuckness'

Why stay at that made-up place?

A short visit is plenty

Invent better

Leave stinky garments in a heap

Come!

Inertia

Inertia.

'Get off yer ass,'

my dad would say

'Make something happen

even if it's wrong' (that is, even if it fails)

        Start. Somewhere. Anywhere.

Letting Go

Lightning bug in a jar

Cannot last long

Lid removed

Let him go

Trail shimmering sparks

all the way to forever

Sprinkling sprinkling still

on us behind

      Quit of you Time

and you Space

capricious jailers both

Current

A *current* as in sea or sky
but without water or mass
A mighty flow of *empty*
that we enter as if a cloudy mist and
realize an overwhelming *presence*
                Dwell there
mindfully
needless
                      And later go off to work
allowing it to flake
on those you meet
Invisible dots of joy

Illusion

Why are some socially adept and others clueless?
A flair of hair, a shape of hip, a curve of smile
all the difference makes
if we subscribe to that world
which we do, mostly
We stack our bricks and drink our portion of wine
      Then again, it is said
what you see – *what you think you see*
is not really how it is –
you are not this body
        You are Love
            and Loved

Form and Formless

It is said God is formless and

also in form

    and is in every breath and cell and action

        and is needless of these

            Every physicality is symbol pointing –

existing as expression

temporary, trying to reach that which is embedded in memory

The memory too is symbol, trying to say what is unsayable

trying to loose the loneliness of separation

Before (Exodus and Jeremiah)

Before I formed you

I know you

I am the air you breathe

and the song before music

I am the shifting wave of every atom

and cool drink on parched sand

I am that I am

and with you always

Staying

A compilation of moments
and stutter steps
Ordinary presence
A spot of compassion

Occasionally tiny bursts of light, hints
of direction, whispers of possibility
like tiny cups of coffee
at a sidewalk café in Paris or Havana

Staying for the long haul, weeding
this ever-demanding garden, discovering only then
purpose and understanding

Grace

When one stumbles in the dark
then sees the outline of a wall
is that goodness or merely dawn?
Perhaps goodness follows us always
and it is up to us to be aware
It is a small matter, but
if we take care of small matters
perhaps the large will fall into place
Let us not be miserable
Let us seek light
Let us *be* light

Positing Faith

My mother was Catholic
My father Lutheran
It seemed normal, though a little odd

Raised Catholic, I was formed
and informed on Thursdays by nuns
in post-WWII Quonset huts, schooled in the faith:
seven of these, five of those, several mysteries, etc.
At home we memorized countless mimeographed truths,
one per day, before we could go out and play baseball

I don't know the difference between what was taught
at Emanual Lutheran down on River Street and what we learned
at St. Alexis out in Willow Run Village

If there is Sin (big S)
it is the pronouncement and embracement of separation
We/they, us/them –
a smallness of mind and heart
an ancient mean-spirited blaming of 'other'

Grandson on Lap

Young grandson on lap

in the dark six A.M.

a quiet gift

As if the Three Wise Men have deposited their load

A brief moment

where all that matters is present

And then he is gone, like a firefly

to the bedroom, under the covers, giggling, cold feet on Nana

Each

Each person is

a crossword puzzle without clue or structure

multi-dimensional

silent yet humming

salty yet bland

pliable

formable and formless, as needed

For each individual a universe created

for each is cherished that much

Acknowledgements

I am thankful to the readers of the original weekly Friday Letters To God for thoughtful notes in response, helping me understand what I was trying to say.

Thanks to BookClub (Martha Daniels, Tom Daniels, Eileen Hatch, Judy Wenzel, Sandy Hines) for decades and decades of discussing and encouraging the written word.

Thanks to Christine Ehrenberg, friend and reader several states away who led me to Debora McNeer, who graciously offered to take on the challenge of making emails and loose pages into book form. Wow.

Thanks to Kerry LaCross for cover art, just stick figures, I said, a five-minute sketch.

Thanks to friend and neighbor Catherine King, faithful Wednesday Editor, whose constant vigilance keeps me looking less foolish.

Thanks to son Luke, a constant Light.

And to my bride, sitting near in the quiet dawn.

Made in the USA
Monee, IL
20 May 2023

2904f629-e7c0-4429-9fc9-eada30e5b07aR01